MW01171606

Replanting My Roots:
A Story of Rescue, Recovery, and Redemption

Published by: Alpha Beta Connections, LLC, In Partnership with
Nia Sadé Akinyemi, *The Literary Revolutionary.*

www.alphabetaconnections.org
www.theliteraryrevolutionary.com

ISBN #: 9781790266265

Copyright © 2018 Shaunella Lee-Brownie

Publisher's Note

Without limiting the rights under copyright reserved above, no part of this
publication may be reproduced, stored in or introduced into a retrieval system,
or transmitted, in any form, or by any means (electronic, mechanical,
photocopying, recording, or otherwise), without the prior written permission of
both the copyright owner and the publisher of the book.

Manufactured in the United States of America

Editing & Cover Design By: *The Literary Revolutionary*
www.theliteraryrevolutionary.com

Follow Author Shaunella
Facebook.com/AlphaBetaConnections
Instagram/Twitter: @alphabetaconnections_llc

www.shaunellabrownie.com

Replanting My Roots:

A Story of Rescue, Recovery, and Redemption

By: Shaunella Lee-Brownie

PUBLISHED IN PARTNERSHIP WITH

The Literary Revolutionary

ATLANTA MIAMI NEW YORK DMV DALLAS

Dedication

...

I would like to dedicate this book to all the men, women, and children who have experienced the lasting effects of domestic violence. Ones who became victorious; and others who became victims. This book is to help you find your silenced voice again. Take your life back! Take territory and replant your roots!

Acknowledgments

...

I give honor to God the Father, who is the head of my life. To my husband, Mark, who encouraged me to push through my pain and write my truth. Coming into my life and showing me the true meaning of love and what a father's love truly looks and feels like for my children. For supporting me 100%... Thank you for making me yours. For breaking through every wall, unlocking my heart, and throwing away the key! My hope is now to pull other victims out of their rut and make them survivors. To my children, who all have been an inspiration to keep fighting and never give up. To my mother, Nellie, who has always been my back bone, showing me from a little girl that those who want it bad enough, work hard for it. If you just believe it, you will achieve it. She always told me, "IF WE GONE BE POOR, WE GONE BE POOR TOGETHER". Family is everything. To my beautiful sister, Ashley, thank you for never giving up on me, even though I gave you plenty of reasons to do so. You were the reason I never felt the pain of never receiving child support. You were their earthly provider and the best T-T alive! Thank you to my Dad, Allen Sr. and his lovely wife, Karen, for always making a way and providing shelter for me and my children. You two have always been a blessing to us. To my oldest brother, Allen Jr., you will always be an inspiration to me; reminding me of our bloodline (Lee/Sconiers), and how we have to be the change we want our children to see. Thank you to my younger brother, Reggie, for stepping up and being a dad to my children, ever since each one came out the womb. For watching them as I worked, and never switching up on me. Thank you for protecting me and fighting for me every time there was an issue. You are the greatest.

Thank you to:

Pastor Rodney and Lady Rhoda Williams;

And church family,

(New Season Christian Church, Indy)

Elder James E. Sullen and Mother Margaret Sullen;

and church family

(Bread OF Life, C.O.G.I.C., Indy)

Pastor Juan and Co-pastor J.E. Clark;

And church family

(The River of Life Community Church, Indy)

All of you have been a part of my journey to help me find my voice.

Last but, not least:

Thank you to my editor and publisher, Ms. Nia Sade Akinyemi, "The Literary Revolutionary".

Because of your book *"Write the Book, Sis!"*

I wrote the BOOK!

Table of Contents

Introduction

•••

One day, you wake up, look around and say, "Why am I here?"

"Am I really homeless this time?"

"What brought me to this place in my life?"

At what point did you decide to come to terms with yourself that living like this was okay? You're in an unfamiliar place! Whether you're living in a shelter, under a bridge, living out of a car, or on a family member's couch – so many questions run through your head and so many emotions fill your mind and body. You think to yourself: who knows I'm here? If they do know I'm here, what are they saying? How will I look to my family? How will my children look at school? You may even say to yourself, ***this is highly EMBARASSING!***

So much runs through your mind and you have an instinct of being strong. I mean after all you've taken your children and yourself through, what else can you be? Yet, at this very moment, if you never knew what being strong looked or felt like before in your life, this is one of your **checkpoints.** Whether you are a mother who has bared children, a woman with adult children, or have no children at all. By just being a **woman**, you experience (at some point) what being ***strong*** really means.

Women have so many hidden talents that we don't know about ourselves; talents that we wouldn't even understand where the abilities come from until a situation arises and we must find it within us to pull it out. We end up fighting to use exactly what we knew or didn't know we had! We are placed into positions where we must make choices. We must choose independence, first and foremost! This decision can **make** or **break** us. We have to choose; do I choose to stay in this rut? Should I throw a pity party with *complimentary* *wine, cheese, and crackers?* Or, will I choose to finally become the woman I always knew I could be?

PAIN

...

I didn't know you could feel that deep.

As I ignore it, it continues to creep.

Pain just choked me out again,

From the strength of its very hands.

It cuts so deep and makes me feel so weak.

As if I can't stand the test of time, I pray

For YOUR will Lord...

Instead of MINE.

Speak Lord Your Servant Is Listening...

Inspirational Reading:

Jeremiah 29: 11 -"For I know the plans I have for you," declares the Lord, "plans to prosper you and not to harm you, plans to give you a future hope and an expected end.

ONE

Uprooting

• • •

Where do I begin?

You may be wondering *who is this woman* and *what credibility does she have that can help lead me out of my dysfunctional lifestyle*? Chile… let me tell you; or better yet, let me reflect.

I could start this chapter talking about the beginning of my domestic violence story; when I felt the first slap from an angry hand that landed me across the room in our closet, all in front of my seven month old first born son. I could also speak about the time my stomach was pushed in and I was thrown down two flights of icy stairs while I was five months pregnant with my second child. Instead, I'll share with you the time I had to stop looking for a savior and finally rescue myself!

It was 2012 and we had just had our third child at this point. I admit it was a very rough and emotional pregnancy, because it took place after our divorce. We planned to get remarried and try it again, so we went downtown and applied for another marriage certificate. After coming home, he left back out to go see his uncle; or at least that's what he said. (Sips Tea)

While he was gone, I received a phone call from one of his family members letting me know he was at a doctor's appointment with another woman. They had just found out she was twelve weeks pregnant! I instantly broke down crying. I couldn't understand what I did to deserve this. I looked down at my already five month pregnant belly and told myself I had to leave. This was straight disrespectful!

My oldest son who was four at the time came into the living room where I was sitting and asked me, "Mommy why you crying? Can I eat-eat?" At that moment, I made the decision to put myself on the back burner and rescue my two babies.

I remember coming up with goals while I walked to the food pantry five blocks away to go get food for my two children to eat. I recall it being such an embarrassing time to carry all those paper bags home; much less my children sharing a stroller and having to put more bags underneath. However, that was the situation considering my ex-husband had taken the car to run the streets, as he often did. We started off young making a family, at the ages of 17 and 18. To him, running the streets at that time was considered "living his best life!" Yet, as a mommy, making sure my children were fed and taken care of was living *my* best life. As I stated before, I knew in order to rescue myself, I needed a plan.

I decided since I had no income and I had decided to leave this toxic relationship, I needed a job! The next morning, I went to the unemployment line and spoke with a counselor. I signed up for Certified Nursing Assistant training that they agreed to pay for! I got my childcare in order (my mother) and started my six week classes. My classes and my children remained my motivation!

After I finally finished, I was hired on as a C.N.A. I was beyond excited. I felt I had gained my independence back! I worked for two months, until I gave birth to my beautiful baby girl.

The day I gave birth, I remember him coming into my hospital room late that night to tell me he was moving out and he would be back once the other woman gave birth! I sat up in the hospital bed and asked him, "What about our family? We have three children now." My ex slapped me so hard, I swear to you I saw stars, as he yelled, "B****, don't question me!" I tried to raise up out of the bed. My body was sore and I was bleeding everywhere. He left out of my room so fast. When I finally got up to go after him, I looked out of my room to see him grab a woman's hand and walk fast to get to the elevator. I was so devastated.

I didn't call for help; I couldn't. I found myself protecting him once again! If I called for help, I knew the hospital would blow it out of proportion and include CPS. I didn't want another case, as we already had plenty over the years. Each time resulted in me dropping the charges.

I grabbed my baby girl out of her bassinet, held her, and told her, "Mommy promises you won't have to grow up seeing that!"

***

My children's father picked us up the next day from the hospital. The drive home was cold and silent. He dropped me off at the door and told me he would be back in a few days to get his clothes. I called the landlord that day and asked her to take him off the lease. She brought the new lease by that day! (**Look at God, Amen!**) Four days later, I walked to the trustee's office requesting assistance, and they paid my rent for two months. I was so grateful.

I received a phone call later from my ex saying he missed his family and that he would be home later that night. I was thinking to myself, *bruh? What home?*

I told him that he was no longer welcomed. His clothes were at his uncle's house where I'd dropped them off after he brought me back our car. I told him to move forward and enjoy his life. Of course that set him off! **(I guess I wasn't supposed to say that…)** I knew he might react, so I immediately planned for our safety.

Before going to bed that night, I pushed my couch in front of my front door. Then, I opened a play pen and wedged it between the back door and the wall. I was confident he couldn't kick my door in! I took my children upstairs to my room; holding my seven day old baby girl, and we laid down to sleep. I placed my car alarm keys under my pillow, just in case.

I remember falling asleep so peacefully, then hearing a creak on the step. I knew somebody was in my house, and I knew it was him. He flung open my bedroom door, and I could see he was enraged. I looked in his eyes before he lunged at me. He seemed like the monster from my childhood nightmares. He ran towards me as I sat up on my mattress bed on the floor. He began choking me saying, "B**** you trying to take away my family?"

By that time, my oldest son woke up and jumped on his back saying, "Get off my momma!" He then let my neck go and told our son to get off his back. He woke up our three year old daughter and told them to take their baby sister in their room because he needed to "talk to mommy". They reluctantly followed directions. Before I could make it to the door, he snatched me by my pony tail and said, "I said we need to talk!"

I knew that day I could die!

My ex slammed our door and he started to punch me in my face. His voice began to drown out in the background as he continued to hit. Then it stopped. He pulled me off the ground and told me to go down stairs. I was so weak from having given birth just seven days before. As I went to the stairs he said, "I don't want the kids hearing us." He semi-carried me out the door.

I remember glancing over through weary eyes at my oldest boy standing in his doorway, stiffening up his upper lip, and balling up his little fist. I guess I was moving too slow, because the next thing I remember is being pushed down those flight of stairs and landing at the bottom. I looked up toward the top, only to see my ex-husband running towards me, and my son now at the top of the stairs holding my new born baby as she slept.

My ex-husband then dragged me across the kitchen floor to the bathroom and told me to get in the tub! I thought, **Oh Lord! He is about to electrocute me!** I laid there on the floor as he stepped over me to close the bathroom window; which I realized was *the way he broke in*! He left me on the bathroom floor and I heard the front door close. I crawled out the bathroom to the back door where my home phone was located. My father had just paid for it to be installed that day. It was divine timing!

I called my mom and told her what was going on. She quickly called my sister on three-way, when I heard the front door slam. He was back. I immediately hid the phone under the stoop it once sat on; being conscious not to hang it up. I got up and tried to walk toward the living room, but my stomach cramped and began to bleed out everywhere! He grabbed me by my neck before I could make it to the living room couch. He said, "Ugh, you a nasty b****; bleeding everywhere and s***!" He then slammed me on the couch and proceeded to punch me until I literally could not feel my face. I passed out and woke up to him saying, "D*mn this bi*** is dead." I moved my head between the couch pillows to soften the blows, but he just kept on hitting.

Then, I heard a voice! I sat straight up and yelled, "Stop!" I listened again and it was my newborn crying. ***Nothing else mattered in that moment.*** I looked at him and he said to go get her and bring her here. I was happy to get away. I went to the steps to see my oldest boy holding my newborn, but he was barely supporting her tiny body. I climbed the stairs to get the baby, and I remembered hearing my son say something so profound that it set my mind back to my goals. He said, "Mommy, please don't die!" ***When I tell you his words rejuvenated my entire body...***

I lifted my baby and found the strength to walk back down the steps. I carried her into the living room where her father remained. I placed my baby down, as I prayed that God would deliver me from this situation. Suddenly, he received a phone call that he placed on speaker. It was a woman's voice claiming she was hungry and missing him at home. He laughed as he told her he was on his way with food. He then hung up the phone, kissed my forehead and said, "Baby, I'll be home in the morning." I tried to turn my hurt face into a grin; just enough for him to leave.

He left the house and I ran straight up the stairs to my kids. I found my oldest son putting on him and his sister's shoes. They were mismatched, but I didn't care. It was clear he and I both were ready to go. I wrapped my newborn up in her receiving blanket and grabbed her portable bassinet. I woke up my three year old and they followed me down the stairs. I went out the front door when the police pulled up.

I remember dropping from exhaustion!

My sister called the police after getting the information from my mother on three way. She didn't know my address, but gave them a description of my place and they found me. That way truly a Godsend.

Soon after, I was being lifted onto a stretcher and was placed into an ambulance. Someone asked me who could take my children. I pleaded with them to just let me go to my mom's house. I remember them letting me get some things and helping me into the car. I saw a few different family members (some not related by blood) pull up, ready for action. They heard about my being beat up and they wanted **BLOOD!** Finally, I was escorted to my mom's house. There I knew it was time to rescue myself.

***

GRIEVANCE

...

Lord I can't bear the pain, please help me.

Everything I worked for I will never see.

Incline your ears unto my heart.

But **PLEASE** don't make me look the part.

You said you would wipe every tear away?

But when will that be, surely not today?

I **YELLED**, I **SCREAMED**, I questioned you.

Hearing Mom's voice, "That's what I shouldn't do"

She taught me to pray and **MEDITATE** day & night.

Like Momma said, "If God took it away…

Don't put up a **FIGHT."**

Speak Lord, for your Servant is listening…

Inspirational Readings:

James 4:9 - Grieve, mourn and wail. Change your laughter to mourning and your joy to gloom.

Matthew 5:4 - Blessed are those who mourn, for they shall be comforted.

Philippians 4:19 - And my God will supply all your needs according to His riches in glory in Christ Jesus.

TWO

Finding My New Start

...

At what point do you say, "I can't call on anybody in my family or I can't sleep on anybody's couch for the night; just to go right back to the situation tomorrow?" I knew in my heart that I had to rescue myself. This time had to be different! I remember time and time again my family sticking their neck out for me and continually helping to pick up the pieces. They would allow me to sleep on their couch or extra room; only to have him banging on their door demanding to see the children.

Many times my father or his wife would buy me a phone, so I could keep in touch. He would break it every time. Imagine your parents losing all hope in you, and they were your strongest support system? I started to feel like I was the butt of all jokes; a true laughing stalk. One time I was truly on the run from him, moving out yet again while he was away. I called my mother to help me move and she refused to come to my rescue because she feared I would just go right back. That was one of the most hurtful feelings.

My dad's wife came and helped me quickly move, and took me to yet another shelter! This one was completely different, more like a phase 1 transitional house/apartment. I gained employment at a fast food restaurant that I walked to daily at 4:00 am to make sure I was on time. My mom would keep my children while I worked. I remember praying as I walked that God would send his "war angels" to protect me as I traveled to and from work. I remember praying for another car, as my ex-husband kept ours.

One day as I was riding the bus back to the shelter, because I was too tired to walk, I saw our car pulled over. I knew it was mine from the distinctive rust marks on the bumper of the car and two unknown men getting arrested on the side of the road! Baby when I tell you I pulled that lever for the bus to stop. I approached the officer and asked about the situation. He informed me the two men were speeding and he found some things on them. They were being detained and the car was being towed. I quickly told him this was my vehicle and showed him my identification.

Oh my GOSH! What Divine intervention! He let me drive off in my car. I went and picked up my babies from my mom's house. God really came through that day, like many other times before.

Sometimes (like in my situation) you must rescue yourself and your children! I had to bring them out of a situation that was no longer providing growth to us. Even though I chose to return on many different occasions; I knew it wasn't aiding us anymore. It took me returning over a span of years, when I finally decided one day that enough was enough. I knew if I didn't leave, I would end up in one of the following three conditions.

1.) Dead.
   (How many times do you have to be choked out or hemmed-up, before you lose your fight?)
2.) Losing custody of all my children.

(How many allegations and home visits will it take before you realize your babies will still be there when you mate walks away?) The children didn't ask to be here, yah know?

3.) In prison, for trying to defend myself. So, I had to create my own option. LEAVE and NEVER go back.

· · ·

TEARS

...

Lord when will they stop?

I try so hard, but I can't CROP

Them out the pictures I Post for people to see.

Pain, Fear and Utter Shock, yet, if they knew

I would become a Mockery of disgust and Grief.

My heart that I wear upon my sleeve.

My Tears keep flowing like the rain, so much heartache

So much PAIN.

So, I will continue to hide in fear....

Keep silence my tears.

As you collect them in a BOTTLE as they fall

WAITING for me to ANSWER your call.

Speak Lord, Your Servant Is Listening...

Inspirational Reading:

Psalms 56:8 - You keep track of all my sorrows. You have collected all my tears in your bottle. You have recorded each one in your book.

Psalms 34: 18-19 - The Lord is close to the broken hearted and saves those who are crushed in spirit. Many are the afflictions of the righteous, but the Lord will deliver them out of them all.

THREE

The Potter is BACK on the Wheel

...

You may ask – when do you know it's time to leave? I encourage you to make a list of your personal pros and cons. Listed below are a few indicators that it's time to reevaluate your situation and make plans to rescue yourself and your children.

When will I know it's time to leave?

1. You're no longer comfortable in the position that you're in.
2. No matter what you do, you're no longer happy.

3. You no longer have that natural glow and the smile that won't go away.

*** *People will let you know something is different about you.* ***

How do I know when to move forward in life? *Some straightforward signs that it is time to leave because the abuse is affecting the children, are below:*

1. Your children's behavior starts to gradually change negatively. ***Story Time***: When my oldest son was in kindergarten, he attempted to commit suicide. Yes, you read that correctly. I got a call from his school and I had to rush him to the children's mental ward! He stayed for five days on suicide watch. It seemed like forever while he was away; visiting him as if he were in jail. All of this was because I kept going back to an abusive situation.

   I remember my son told the therapist, he felt like his father would return home if he was no longer alive. He felt as if he was hated. I never asked my children how they felt every time I allowed him back in, thinking I was putting my family back together. That was the hardest thing to accept as a mom.

2. They show introverted characteristic traits when they once were extroverted.
3. They don't want to play as much.
4. They develop separation anxiety.
5. They seem more timid and fearful.

*** *Trust me, if a child is living in fear, they will tell someone outside of the home. It's best you step while you still have the option!* ***

At the end of the day, Mommy is always **Superwoman.** Mommy is always the **savior** of the problem or situation. When our children bump their heads, skin a knee, or have a bad dream, who do they call? What if you're the only one making their dreams a reality? By choosing daily to stay in an abusive relationship, we are absentmindedly bringing the **monster** right to our front door.

What else could be a clear sign?

When things that you could once hold together so well just starts falling apart; you find yourself trying to hold onto things and it's literally out of your control. Everything goes downhill. Bills, housework, and stress pile up. You try and try and TRY! You fight and fight, yet nothing seems to work.

FEER

...

God didn't give me the SPIRIT of Fear,

And I know that to be true.

But where is God when I'm standing in front of you?

Do I push past you, as If you don't exist?

Yet, your words haunt me and leave a

Sticky mist.

Too **scared** to go forward, too **PROUD** to look back.

So, I will stand still and remember my LACK.

I'm not good enough or have the wrong body type.

My hair is too short, and my curves don't look right!

I know you hate me and that's what I fear about you.

Because without love in your heart….

God only knows what you will do!

Speak Lord; Your Servant is Listening…

Inspirational Readings:

Isaiah 41: 10 - So do not fear, for I am with you; do not be dismayed, for I am your God. I will strengthen you and help you; I will uphold you with my right hand.

2 Timothy 1:7- For the Spirit God gave us does not make us timid, but gives us power, love and self-discipline.

FOUR

Resting in the Master's Hands

...

When we lean into our own understanding, we're not allowing ourselves to trust the process. Thus, we have to continue going through the same exact problem and test over and over again. That is until a lightbulb goes off in our heads and you says, "Let me do this another way, because it is insane that I keep getting the same outcome." It took me having to experience homelessness five times; three shelters and living with family; sleeping on their floors and basements for me to finally get it.

One day, I remember waking up to a flooded basement and scrambling to get my oldest son, who wasn't even one year old at the time, and myself out. I lost the little bit of clothing I had in that situation. The homelessness started when my oldest son was a year old, back in 2009 and ending when I had my 3rd child in 2012. In 2009 I didn't know it was going to take three year later, for me to say enough is enough. I'm not going back. I'm not doing the same cycle over. I'm going to take charge of my life. I'm going to redeem myself with the public, with my family, and most importantly, with the woman that I must look at in the mirror daily. I began to think… *What am I going to tell my children? What type of legacy am I going to leave behind? What type of example am I going to set for my daughters?*

Listen…

There's nothing wrong with going to a shelter. In fact, to leave a deadly or selfish situation, it may be key! Whether it's an abusive relationship or being surrounded with the wrong crowd. I've been in more than one before, where some were physically abusive and others were mentally or financially abusive. Whether you're dealing with relationships involving drugs or being into something that could intentionally take you away from the ones who love you the most. This could potentially leave you with consequences to deal with for a lifetime. What if you staying meant for protective services to remove your children from the home, putting you through an obstacle course, just to make you a qualifying candidate, to receive YOUR OWN CHILDREN BACK! I've been through this, all because I chose to stay with an unstable abusive man.

Maybe it could be a sudden bomb in your life and everything changes within minutes! For instance, you could be working a fantastic job heading toward retirement, and out of nowhere you get wrongfully fired! You don't know which way to turn. How will the bills get paid? Your nest egg only has so much in it. After that savings runs out, what now? You find yourself too "seasoned" to work. (We aren't going to say "old". We're going to say "seasoned".) Maybe housekeeping was all you knew how to do; working as a maid or in hotels. Maybe you were a C.N.A. all your life, and patient care is all you know at this point. Maybe you were a waiter/waitress, or fast food crew member! Yet, now you can no longer lift or bend like you used too; or you can't walk or stand long hours like you were once able to do seamlessly. Now things are different, and companies aren't impressed by your work history or loyalty to one job field.

No one is blowing your phone up to hire you. Your resume is no doubt at the bottom of the DO NOT HIRE pile.

Let's just say you find a job. Now you're at a lower paying job, and can barely make ends meet. You find yourself having to save face and go to a shelter! You pack up your lovely dream home and leave all your memories behind. Even in the midst of that unpredictable storm, rescuing yourself from that blockage in life is one of the best decisions in life you can make! Choosing to step out on faith and see the first time around what God has in store for you… One step toward a new life, will bring the determination you need to recover all that you have lost! I dare you take that step. Don't be the one who didn't get away. Another tragic end in the TOP NEWS stories **because you love him**.

It could also be the fact I don't want others to know I'm homeless, so we pretend as if everything is ok. You will succeed if you follow these simple steps and just take heed to your SURROUNDINGS!! Yes, it took me five times to leave the comfort of my own home to understand. I was being completely selfish to my children; for continuing to return to a marriage that was unhealthy for us as a whole. It clearly wasn't ordained by God for me to be there.

You can choose to disobey God, but after so long he will allow things to happen. (**ROMAN 1:28**) You have to make up in your mind to not look back. My going back wasn't about the children or finances. It was me, straight up being stiff-necked and stubborn, though every time the children weren't in a physically dangerous household. It was mentally draining and flat-out abuse. Calling me demeaning names in front of our children and beating me up to the point of bruising and bleeding; leaving me to clean up the mess that was left after every fight, daily. It started to become a storyline; different beginnings with the same outcome. It was always me leaving my home to try and defuse the situation. It just got worse and worse overtime. One day it clicked. I was like, "Nah, it's time to go!" I know it's something else out there for me to achieve. I dare you to stop looking around and look on the mirror.

You can leave in the middle of the night, when you feel the time is right! It may be when you have just fed your children, just paid what you could towards rent and put in your 30-day notice. Be smart about it. If you can, don't leave stones unturned. Don't get evicted! Pay what you can, then put in a 30-day notice of "vacay", meaning you are leaving or vacating the property and the owner's property will be empty. It's time to swallow that hard pill of PAIN, and take that first step! Leave out that door and go to the "safe haven". Go to the shelter, that's what they are there for. They are there to help you get back on your feet. They are not designed for you to stay and live for the rest of your life. They are designed to be a stepping stone to SUCCESS!

•••

SILENCE

...

I mustn't speak, he said don't tell a soul.

So, to keep **SILENT** is my goal.

Though my heart breaks with every question you ask. I will remain focused and steadfast.

Please I need you, can't you hear me crying. If you saw through this act you could see that I'm dying.

Mouth pressed shut, with so many memories to review. I can't help but remember you.

What you did was wrong on so MANY levels. Every time you showed up it was a new devil.

I've grown tired of fighting and now I give it to the **MASTER** to keep. As I enter my secret place just to **WEEP**.

I will keep silent and pray to God to save me.

Take away this abuse and pain that my heart can no longer obtain.

Speak Lord, Your Servant is Listening…

Inspirational Readings:

Isaiah 41: 10 - So do not fear, for I am with you; do not be dismayed, for I am your God. I will strengthen you and help you; I will uphold you with my right hand.

2 Timothy 1:7 - For the Spirit God gave us does not make us timid, but gives us power, love and self-discipline.

FIVE

Laying a New Foundation

• • •

"Still not convinced...? That there's Sunshine on the other side of the storm?"

Again, trust me, I know what you are going through. You know it's time to leave when you predict the pain. Even if you're a seasoned woman and you are left alone to start a new life for yourself, sitting in a living room stressed out as bills continue to pile on top of you. Going further into debt. Beginning to run out of local resources and wondering where you can turn. Knowing the eviction notice will definitely be the end all - tell all for your story. To make matters worse, the bank has moved to foreclosure on you dream home, that you have dwelled in for so long. They aren't just taking your home, but the memories left behind for those happy times in you and your family's life.

You break down and have to possibly file bankruptcy... if that's even an option. Now you don't make enough to cover your cars or dream house you once had. You have so much debt and bill collectors that bring nothing but stress! You don't want to continue to stress and end up with hypertension (high blood pressure) or a heart attack or even as stroke, like my mother experienced. You could also develop anxiety and depression through this whole STUBBORN process! You are not alone, you can do this! IT IS POSSIBLE!

You are probably asking yourself by now; if I were to leave today, where would I go? Well, I'm so glad you decided to ask. Let me help you with that.

Remember to always be smart about it. Call around to different shelters in advance. See who has room. Also call your local resource connections line. (For Indiana, it is likely #211) While on the phone ask them to call the shelter for you and act as an advocate to bridge the gap. This will allow the shelters to take the situation more seriously. A resource line can also later help with paying utilities, paying rent, and finding food pantries. They are put in place to help you help yourself and to come to terms that ENOUGH IS ENOUGH! You want better in life.

PAUSE!!

WAYMENT…. HOLLUP?!

Imagine waking up 20 years from now dealing with the same old' mess while you're watching your peers and friends flourish and thrive all around you; maturing into successful adults while you're still standing on the bus stop. Instead of paying off a car or paying off a house or even graduating college/technical school, educate yourself past high school. You want to push forward and show yourself first and foremost, that you can do it. Then you want to show others around you that you can accomplish your set goals. Best believe someone is watching you. Somebody is mentally recording your story! It may be your child that is watching your every move that you make. It could be your mother or father who believe that you can do so much better.

Maybe it's a peer from school who happens to follow you on social media. There is always somebody watching you. They are wondering when you are going to snap out of it. When are you going to believe you deserve better? You can get all the "likes" and you're still lonely or next to your abuser. You lay there with your mind wandering in social media world. Stop dreaming and be what you imagine to be. Don't stay for "false love"; men and women alike. Men go through challenging times, too. Women can abuse men, also.

I have lost two friends to suicide, both showed signs of relationship abuse. They were being told they weren't good enough. Women threatening to take the kids away. Meanwhile, the father is doing their best to provide. Don't hurt yourself, just leave the situation and strive to do better.

• • •

SHOCK

...

I can't believe you! Are you for real?

I thought this time we had a deal?!

You won't hurt me just to make them smile. Yes, I know it's been awhile.

Come hold me and tell me everything's ok! Yet, you leave me alone in disarray?!

To pick up my face from off the ground;

Right in the mud is where it's found.

Lord please reveal to me what this means?

Cause I learned a LONG time ago….

Everything's NOT what it SEEMS.

Speak Lord; Your Servant is listening…

Inspirational Reading:

Psalms 8:2 - Through the praise of children and infants you established a stronghold against your enemies, to silence the foe and the avenger.

Psalms 115:17 - It is not the dead who praise the Lord, those who go down to the place of silence.

SIX

Buried Deep

•••

Now that you've left, it's time to RECOVER! *(PAUSE... TAKE A PRAISE BREAK. OMG, YOU LEFT!!!! GOOD JOB!)*

Okay, I'm back. You rescued yourself from the WAR in that relationship and unfulfilling lifestyle. You took that step and secured your spot in the "safe haven" or shelter. It's time to heal your mental and physical wounds. Time to get yourself together and RECOVER! After losing all your belongings and having to leave valuable things behind, no matter if it's clothes or kid's toys (because that matters with their mental stability). It could be your money that you left because you had to run for your life, with only the clothes on your back. Even the "seasoned" women who had to leave their property, because of eviction foreclosed. Maybe, you couldn't afford a storage. Thinking to yourself, you once were somebody and now you are a nobody in this world. Maybe, your social status has dropped. Now you're at the shelter because you took a hard turn for the worst! Yet, for you it's **likely** for the best. As you sit and ponder and really think about it, it's time to bring that Superwoman OUT! Let's make a game plan! Write it out! Figure it out:

- How long do they (the shelter) allow you to stay there?

- Do they offer child care? If not, where is the nearest childcare facility?

- Who is hiring?

- Do you have income? Can you apply for housing?

- Do they offer transportation assistance?

That's just a few questions to get you started. Don't get lazy! This isn't the time to just chill! Understand when you're no longer your own boss, it will bring out a lot of emotions. I'm warning you ahead of time, so it doesn't take you by surprise. If you go through this TEST correctly you will see your TESTIMONY. You may find yourself snapping on the Social Worker or Case Manager at the shelter. Remember even if you may think they are snobby or stuck –up, continue to ask for resources. That is a part of their job, to help you. Remember they don't have to be here helping you. They are leaving their family to dedicate themselves to this job title.

Part of RECOVERY is finding yourself again: Learning how to feel gorgeous again, learning to dress for less, attend church or social groups again. Here some ideas:

1. Go to a local Beauty School and get your hair done for little or no money, instead of going to the beauty shop.

2. Try the up & coming nail techs to keep your nails done for less. (You can also find them at the beauty school.) Take pride in how you carry yourself again.

3. Begin to seek childcare, if you have children. Go to the local "Social Services" office, ask about job search

classes, and assistance in childcare. If there is a waiting list get on it. Also, apply for cash assistance!

4. Go sign up for college courses and grants. I'm not advising you to rack up on student loans, but advise a plan and **STICK TO IT!**

5. You could start job searching. Never be too prideful at your starter jobs. You need a paycheck, period. You'll be able to move out the shelter sooner.

I'm telling you this, so you don't have to come back to the shelter three or four times. Don't make it a permanent housing plan. Again, the shelter is designed to help you get back on your feet! It's one stepping stone to get to the next stepping stone! Make sure you follow the rules and don't overstep your boundaries. Then, you will see progress.

•••

DISGUST

...

The thought of you DISGUST me to an angry extent.

The sound of your name makes me cringe.

What's worst seeing you in the mirror? Or knowing what you did?

Both makes me want to grab a bag and repeatedly GAG! –

Up my feelings for you that I should not have had!

Every tear of disgust as it falls down my face,

Stings my cheeks

As if it were MACE! You knew better to trust them, you even had the evidence to see. The mental and emotional scars, left on me. Throw me into the SEA OF FORGETFULLNESS,

And hopefully not close to the shore!

I vowed to make a change, this woman you know, will be NO MORE!

Speak Lord; Your Servant is listening…

Inspirational Reading:

Ecclesiastes 2:2 - "Laughter", I said, "is madness. And what does pleasure accomplish?"

Psalms 23:1-6 – The Lord is my shepherd, I lack nothing. He makes me lie down in green pastures, he leads me besides quiet waters, He refreshes my soul. He guides me along the right paths for his name's sake. Even though I walk through the darkest valley, I will fear no evil, for you are with me; your rod and your staff, they comfort me. You prepare a table before me in the presence of my enemies. You anoint my head with oil; my cup overflows. Surely your goodness and love (mercy) will follow me all the days of my life, and I dwell in the house of the Lord FOREVER.

SEVEN

It's Cold and Lonely Down Here

...

After you have secured childcare, find a job. You want to establish an income, as soon as you can! You could find a local military recruiter and join the Armed Forces. You could be active duty (full time job and pay) or National Guard (part time job and pay). I joined the Army National Guard. It was a great decision in my life and for my children. It allows me to serve my country and earn respect from the world. Also, it has opened doors for getting my degree as they will pay for your classes. I have regular pay monthly and no, I didn't have to lose custody of my children to join and leave for training.

Otherwise, many restaurants are hiring. Being a server is also nice. Being able to bring home tips after work, so you can make ends meet throughout the week. After you secure the job, go apply for the next upcoming semester in schooling. It should be free or close to nothing if you use your resources. Therefore, you can be on you job long enough before you start as a student. After starting school, continue to work just as hard; don't slack NOW! When you are apply for housing they usually look for you to make three times the rent amount monthly. That means if rent is $500.00, you need to bring in at least $1,500.00 monthly. After you have been working for 30 days or more, start applying for housing. Go to all the low-income housing apartments first. Even if they have a waitlist, you will be PRIORITY! You must explain to them you're homeless, yet you have income. Also, apply for homes in your income range. Go online and look for homes. Let the landlord know your situation and provide a letter of "homelessness", from your case manager; showing you are really in a shelter. Sometimes, like in my case, apartments will take a letter of intent to hire or something showing your start date and pay rate. Make sure you start in just a few days, not weeks away.

As I said before, go to your local community college. Sign up for classes and go part-time, at least. You can also go visit your local unemployment office and sign up for a technical or certification class. Your goal is to gain independence BEFORE you are truly INDEPENDENT! You will have a new beginning, if you put your mind to it.

Finally, turn to God. You need to be obedient to him and learn his words. Receive the precious gift of salvation. Get to know him for yourself; learn what it means to "plead the blood over the situation"; the blood that was shed on the cross, from Jesus sacrificing his life, so we can be free. The blood covers all sin and protects you. Find a local church home, so you can have "covering" over yourself, family, and life. Believe in yourself. Attend church every time the doors are opened if you can! Fellowship is good for the soul. That's what worked for me.

Go to work. Don't miss ANY days, no matter how you feel. Take your children to childcare, so you have no excuses! Understand, this is the RECOVERY PERIOD. It's the time to GRIND like you never have done before and make it happen. Remember every morning you must leave the shelter. You might as well be doing something productive while you're away from the babies. Curfew will soon get on your nerves, because you could be at your own home, with your own rules.

• • •

PEACE

I'm pacing back and forth

Can't sit down. Looking for signs that won't be found.

Talking on the phone and;

reading books to help me sleep.

But still haven't heard a PEEP.

You say patience is a virtue and I read it in **your** word.

But why is my mind against it, as if it's UNHEARD.

I will PATIENTLY wait for time to pass,

But I promise I'm like a student;

the night before a new class.

Eager and ready to show the world **his** plan.

As for now it will remain in the **MASTER'S** Hand.

Speak Lord Your Servant Is Listening...

Further Reading:

Matthew 18:21-35- 21 Then Peter came to Jesus and asked, "Lord, how many times shall I forgive my brother or sister who sins against me? Up to seven times?"

22 Jesus answered, "I tell you, not seven times, but seventy-seven times.

23 "Therefore, the kingdom of heaven is like a king who wanted to settle accounts with his servants. 24 As he began the settlement, a man who owed him ten thousand bags of gold was brought to him. 25 Since he was not able to pay, the master ordered that he and his wife and his children and all that he had be sold to repay the debt.

26 "At this the servant fell on his knees before him. 'Be patient with me,' he begged, 'and I will pay back

everything.' 27 The servant's master took pity on him, canceled the debt and let him go.

28 "But when that servant went out, he found one of his fellow servants who owed him a hundred silver coins. He grabbed him and began to choke him. 'Pay back what you owe me!' he demanded.

29 "His fellow servant fell to his knees and begged him, 'Be patient with me, and I will pay it back.'

30 "But he refused. Instead, he went off and had the man thrown into prison until he could pay the debt. 31 When the other servants saw what had happened, they were outraged and went and told him everything that had happened.

32 "Then he called the servant in. 'you horrible servant,' he said, 'I canceled all that debt of yours because you begged me to. 33 Shouldn't you have had mercy on your fellow servant just as I had on you?' 34 In anger his master handed him over to the jailers to be tortured, until he should pay back all he owed.

35 "This is how my heavenly Father will treat each of you unless you forgive your brother or sister from your heart."

EIGHT

Lord Is That Your Voice I Hear?

...

Time to take authority in your life again. Like I stated before, I joined the Army as a point to take authority over my life. I came from an abusive relationship and I had to regain AUTHORITY in my life.

So, you're finally in your own place! **(Whoop – Whoop! Excellent Job; see I told you could do it.)** Now, it's time to shut all the haters and distractions out and focus. Shut the mouths of your enemies that talked about you and prayed for your downfall. Make yourself credible again to society, your family, and more importantly yourself! Start looking for places that offer resources on furniture and kitchen ware. Trust me there are plenty of free furniture places to fix up your new place. Call your local connections resource line. You should also look online for "cars for cash" and purchase one for $1000.00 or less. Just until you can leap to the next stepping stone.

Next, apply for a low cash limit credit card. Securing that card in your name will begin to build your credit properly. For example, if the card credit limit is $300.00, only spend $50.00. Pay that off in two months, not all at once. Watch what that does to your credit score, even with something as small as that. Continue to do this and never spend more than $125.00 out of that $300.00. That will keep what they call a "credit utilization rate" down. If you happen to spend the whole $300.00 and miss a payment or can't pay it. At least pay it down to .30% of the credit limit so it doesn't damage your score. Remember don't spend, just because you have it on your card.

Next, you should open a checking and savings account. Sign up for direct deposit from you job. Set up an automatic transfer for $25.00 (or more) to be taken out of your checking account and placed into your savings account every pay day. You won't see it come out unless you look.

Therefore you won't miss it. Thus, you begin to build your nest egg. The nest will be there to help buy a better car, to get car repairs, and help pay off credit cards for emergency money when needed. Doing these straightforward steps will give you another chance at a successful life.

REVELATION

...

WOW! That's deep! My eyes are open now.

Learned information, but in books it can't be found.

I woke up from a vision and agreed to the NEW MISSION.

I'm smarter, wiser, filled with new AMBITION! He said,
"WRITE THE VISION AND MAKE IT PLAIN"!

Not for awards or any fame.

This is between me and the Heavenly Father.

I'm glad he ENTRUSTED it with me,

When this seed matures, then the entire world will see!

Standing bright and tall. People wondering how I didn't
fall.

Because when he gave me the VISION... I wrote it down.

Never told a soul, my face to the ground.

Inspirational Readings:

James 4:9 - Grieve, mourn and wail. Change your laughter to mourning and your joy to gloom.

Matthew 5:4 - Blessed are those who mourn, for they shall be comforted.

Philippians 4:19 - And my God will supply all your needs according to His riches in glory in Christ Jesus.

-TIME TO EMERGE-

At the end of the day, as you lay there scared not knowing where you are going to sleep tonight or who you can borrow money from to pay the bill... Wondering how you're going to avoid this fight because this is usually the night he/she comes home drunk and wants to fight... I want you to look to heaven and say a prayer. Say, "Lord, strengthen me as I proceed on this journey." If not today or tomorrow, make it in the next few days. I want you to take that step of faith and leave! It doesn't matter if you are accepted into the shelter and you don't have your own room yet. Maybe you must sleep in the "overflow" room with other families in your same situation. At least you took that step. Yes, it's going to be hard! Yes, you will want to go back to that dysfunctional place called home, especially if you left from abuse and you still blindly love him. Some days you may feel the stress of finding housing or child care. The job search may be a lengthy process. Sometimes you will have to face the fact that your child is still hungry at night, because he played with his food when the shelter served dinner, and the child doesn't understand no more food for tonight. Many shelters don't allow food in your rooms, unless you're in transitional housing. Use this factor as motivation to get your own place. Someday, your babies will have their own room and a kitchen full of goodies just for them. You will make your own rules again, and stop anyone who tries to take away your independence again. Think about your FREEDOM.

REDEEM yourself.

Heal yourself!

Above all; RESCUE YOURSELF.

JUST LEAVE!

RELIEF

...

I found comfort upon the pages,

In the 66 books that explained my WAGES.

You said you would lighten the LOAD, through the
GREATEST STORY

Ever told.

I take a deep breath and smile.

I see the sun and feel its beams;

I haven't felt that in a while.

You are my burden Barrier.

Give my worries to you, there is no ~~ERROR!~~

I'm confident now, because you have lifted.

Now I can have RELIEF, now my life has SHIFTED

Speak Lord, Your Servant is Listening...

Further Reading:

Matthew 11:28-30- 28 "Come to me, all you who are weary and burdened, and I will give you rest. 29 Take my yoke upon you and learn from me, for I am gentle and humble in heart, and you will find rest for your souls. 30 For my yoke is easy and my burden is light."

Psalms 55:22 - Cast your cares on the Lord

And he will sustain you;

He will never let

The righteous be shaken

Philippians 4:13 - I can do all this through him who gives me strength.

LAUGHTER

...

It's funny how, just last week I had to bow;

To pride and fear.

Couldn't even began to PHATEM that you were NEAR!

I see joy in situations that I once saw SORROW.

That loss was a gain; my hope for TOMMORROW!

I giggle and smile as if to flirt, with my passion and your
POWER;

It gives me SELF-WORTH. So, Laughter is the hammer....

To break down the walls.

I will keep POUNDING... until they FALL!

Speak Lord; Your Servant is listening...

Further Reading:

Job 8:21 - He will yet fill your mouth with laughter

And your lips with shouts of joy.

JOY

...

Who knew life could be so SWEET!

My smile reflects my joy as I take a LEAP-

Of faith knowing it will all soon fade. As of right now

My mind is made-

Up and convinced that this is IT!

New joy, peace and CONFIDENCE!

You can't take my joy away, not now....

OR any other day!

I deserve this and all its GLORY.

You can have joy too

If you knew the PURPOSE

OF MY STORY!

Speak Lord, Your Servant is Listening…

Further Reading:

1 Chronicles 29:17 - I know, my God, that you test the heart and are pleased with integrity. All these things I have given willingly and with honest intent. And now I have seen with joy how willingly your people who are here have given to you.

Job 33:26 - then that person can pray to God and find favor with him,

They will seek God's face and shout for joy;

He will restore them to full well-being.

Psalms 16:11 - You make known to me the path of life;

You will fill me with joy in your presence,

With eternal pleasures at your right hand.

About the Author

...

Shaunella Lee-Brownie is the Owner of Alpha Beta Connections and Author of her new book, "Replanting My Roots: A Story of Rescue, Recovery, and Redemption". She helps bring awareness to the lasting effects of domestic violence by providing resources and facilitating workshops; ultimately helping survivors find their voice in their silence. She is a proud member of the Army National Guard, wife, and mother of five; who wrote this book (her personal story and strategies) to encourage victims of domestic violence to learn how to rescue themselves out of their situation, recover from the traumatic experience, and redeem themselves back into society.

40708806R00057

Made in the USA
Columbia, SC
15 December 2018